The
Breath
of the
Crowd

By the same author

Poems

Don't Exaggerate

Plays

Claw
The Love of a Good Man
Fair Slaughter
That Good Between Us
The Hang of the Gaol
The Loud Boy's Life
Crimes in Hot Countries
Downchild
No End of Blame
Victory
The Power of the Dog
A Passion in Six Days
Scenes from an Execution
The Castle
Women Beware Women
The Bite of the Night

Film

The Blow

Howard Barker

The Breath of the Crowd

JOHN CALDER : LONDON
RIVERRUN PRESS : NEW YORK

First published in Great Britain, 1986, by
John Calder (Publishers) Limited,
18 Brewer Street, London W1R 4AS

And in the United States of America, 1986, by
Riverrun Press Inc
1170 Broadway
New York, NY 10010

All performing rights in 'The Breath of the Crowd' are strictly reserved and applications for performance should be made to:

Judy Daish Associates Limited
83 Eastbourne Mews, London W2 6LQ

No performance of this poem may be given unless a licence has been obtained prior to rehearsal.

British Library Cataloguing in Publication Data

Barker, Howard
    The breath of the crowd
    1. Title
    821'.914   PR6052.A6485
    ISBN 0—7145—4099—4

Printed in Great Britain by Delta Press, Hove.

For

Marylyn Thomas

Prologue

They'd bolt the past into a drawing room
If they could

Smother the yelps of a triumphant reason
In the hems of dresses

And the clots of inspiration mop up
In the flannel of an actor's shirt

So it behoves us

At moments of false celebration
At moments of imminent colonialism
And selective memory

To reach through

The cities of print
The forests of film
The drowning sheets of bands

Bursting the teeth of the star
Breaking the grin of the celebrity

And bawling over the applause
Which draws the pebbles down the beach
And draws them up again

Describe

Our
    strata
        of
           pains
               on
                  pains
Our
    silt
      of
         panics

Obscure
        crucifixions
            and
              unpublished
                  griefs

Europe's deeps

1

The man with the evasive eye
The man whose laugh comes always late
 Speaks with himself

Whether peeling potatoes under the grating
Or staring for fleets on the groyne

The man without religion
Haunts the empty church

Dragging his fingers over the bench
And counting his heel on the tiles

He is imagining the state of being alone

What do you think silence is
Only the absence of sound?

He carries silence in his heart
As the nun in the African mission
Dreams of a Baltic lover

2

I was the crowd's child also
Also the city's son
My mother's cardboard walls
Failed in their filtering
Her discriminations
Her bans
Fell like fabrics into holes
Died like banners in the aisles

I nourished the horror of others
I polished the pain with my sleeve
The pebble in my gut was
A grain in the oyster's bowel
The secretions of which made pearl
Of curiosity

Absurd love of the vagrant
And the unwashed woman

3

Always counter to the street
Oblique to the thoroughfare
For especially in cities you may
Travel contrary to tides

I crouched in the shimmering railway yard

All
    those
        heavy
            heads of
                ragwort

The worm had the sleepers in caves
The rust on the axelbox shoaled
To the finger's exploration

I licked the paint from the truck
Which was condemned

Unutterable passion
Clandestine hunger

Intimacy I reserved for the rot
Of the public thing

The lingering print of the crowd
I searched in secret hours

As the pants of the unknown woman
I salvaged from the shade of the bench

4

The wind blew down the city
Laden as a tram

Carrying the cry of the martyr to the suburbs

The wind shook the sash of the club
Where politics were glued
As the wafer is jammed to the toffee

And the door of the coalhole where
The infant died
It sawed that too

It sawed
It whipped

The galvanized sheet they had bolted
To the mouth of the church

It whipped the skirt of the wife
Whose womb was aflame
And ridiculed the trousers of Americans

How many breaths in a gale?

5

To copulate in a public place may pass for adventure in a
society where risk has been minimized in the interests of
welfare and polar explorers are considered absurd

The woman who was no longer young

Mercifully no longer young

Not burdened with opinion

             borrowed

             chanted

             coagulated

             opinion

Whose eye was wilder with the

Deterioration of the state

Whose lip was kinder with the

Cracking of the edifice

Drew up her skirt

Her skirt which was a well

As dark and bottomless as wells

For his eyes only on the train

The sheer flatness

The unrelieved monotony of plain

Bellied past the window

Slow as fat

Thick as grease

Tankers at the crossing

Pigs in thistles

Troops in holes

He grew at her audacity

As the balding and the coiffured

Oscillated in their privacies

       the child crying

       the Jew reciting

       the rattling kip of the old

She unhitched

She disordered

She exposed

The obscure rhythm of hair and flesh

For which all contoured clothing

Strata of silk or padded bone

Is metaphor

And copulating

They

Beat

Back

The clammy cold of a polite democracy

The crowd is a lie

The turbulence of the hooligan

The manners of the concourse

9

Both a lie

The riot

The rigidity of the congregation

Lies also

Standing next to a stranger you are required

To leave a seven inches' gap and whilst it is

Permitted to look him in the eye two seconds

Is the maximum duration of the stare before

ANTAGONISM or INSANITY set in

Your leg may touch mine if

Your breath may fall upon my cheek but only

You may press your buttock to the stranger's

Groin provided

Shall I take like a thumb print in wax

The shape of the stranger's hip?

10

Look, I am still red from his pressure

She says alone before the mirror

6

I lay alone on the hotel bed

And the hotel craned over the kerb

Inquisitive

Impertinent

As if the medieval craved the kiss

Of upper floors

Abhorring space

(They were fewer and more ashamed)

As if no window felt secure

Without it stared into another

(They feared the view, the wolfpack

On the boundary)

And every intimacy was within

Reach or hearing of domestic doing

The urgent promise whispered to the

        dogbark

        goatbleat

        or the beat of bins

I lay and listened to the women

Naked and white in the breeze

I listened to encumbered women

Narrate the slipping of life

The sickness

The horror of treatment

The comedy of economy

Explicit in the price of vegetables

They hummed their reappearance

They proclaimed they had not died in the night

And the animal cry of their laughter

Clawed to the gutter and roosted

7

The garden of the poet near Salonica
In the interrogation of the moon
Lay still and white as china in
The cabinet
Fine china that moves
Only to the whirr of wings
Or pings to the glance of his sandal
As he walked out sleeplessness

    The pond
    The sabres of the irises
    The bloom's tense wait

The poet had renounced all company
Even the lip of the waitress

And feeling the want of the waitress
The world of her knee
He lay and strained at the funnel of stars
On the stone white bench
He golloped the silence of stars

And it went

(Oh, it goes
There is nothing
Nor grief nor delight
Does not withdraw its sting at last)

His garden bench a writhing tablet
He lay alone

14

Stone

Perfectly stone

They brought food to his gate
(By arrangement)
Passing it under the iron
So he saw not the bringer
Only the basket

His walls were higher than a tall man's head
And his windows opened into a yard
Sparing him the pain of knowing
Even in this remoteness
Some persisted in passing
Some were born on corners
Some died in earshot

And clots of beggars who chucked
Down their sticks
And laughed to unburden their litter
(The contents of their bundles always
Had offended him)
Were flogged to the next place
(By arrangement)

In this concentration upon self
(He kept frogs in the pond
But only to record their depravity)
The poet achieved whole truths

Seized out of his depths
Amazement
Like the man who plunged his raw hand
In the rivers and threw out heavy carp

15

Flapping on the bank
Greater and greater truths
It took both arms to land

But his bread maker
    his beggar chaser
    his mender of walls
Sensing the poet's wealth
Feeling the children's hunger
Pushed the crippled to his gate
Urging them to shrillness
To clatter at all hours
And showed secretly the weak place
In the wall so they might
Fling in pebbles
And spoil the hermit's peace

So his avarice broke the poet's concentration
Demanding more to keep away the mob
He secretly assembled

By what right
Do you disdain us
Since silence
Which is where you travel
(Walking the perimeter of the garden
Was by virtue of discovery
More adventure than explorers
Found in several continents)
Silence
Is privilege and costly

So read the agent's note
Slipped in with the loaves

The poet's fortune spent
            the wall fell
            the food ceased
            and beggars rich
            in impertinence
Crouched among his flowers
Quarrelling inanely
Laughing unhealthily
Fucking ungainly
And urinating on the frogs

This earthquake of flesh
No wisdom prepared him for
No insight armed him against

And the moon
Which had blazed on his solitariness
And cauterized his hungers
Laughed along with Lazarus

BY WHAT RIGHT

He hanged himself with a cord
Borrowed from the
Gambler With The Single Leg

This request to phrase and deliver
Took draughts of energy
And soddened his vest

In the veil of mosquito night
His corpse revolved
Persistently rejecting
Turning its back
Again and again

17

BY WHAT RIGHT

As for his truths
His terrible truths
Inscribed in a perfect hand

These scrolls running to
More than a hundred
Were taken by cart to the city
Where scholars
Weary with defeat
And shamed at sudden impotence
Declared
Them
Incomprehensible

8

All this talk of mortality
All this combing of the cemetery
The family outing to the charnelhouse
The scraping of the moss with the knife
And palsied poets in the porch

The dead are so attractive now
It passes for sensibility
To tread their bits

The girl lay the length of the tomb
The boy urged her naked
Laughing she rinsed her hair in ivy
And her arse outstared the elm
Her belly to the cool hieroglyphic
Her jaw to the iron

What is the dead man's slab but an
Imperative
His titles are only rebukes

The quarrel of the cemetery we cannot hear
The roar the beating of bones the butcher
Stuffed between his widow the confectioner
Whose pelvis cracked under the coffin of the
Thief

And soldiers' graves are drilling stones

9

He flings up his sash

Bald man

    with

        more

           time

              than

                  imagination

He hates clocks

Their lethargy

And immobile hands

He trod his watch to pieces in a sleepless night

For showing only five minutes had elapsed since his

Last look

But one on a tower chimes the hours

Unbelievably late each one

And all his nocturnal visits

Armed with bricks don't crack its face

The bricks fall back to earth

And then the dogs get barking

All the night etcetera

The lights the blinds etcetera

Drive him back in

The stir of the pack rekennels him

He flings up his sash

Bald man

      with

         neither

            love

               nor

                  power

He hears a woman's heels

Go beating down the street

Not unlike clockwork

She possesses a destination

In this she's rich

Or is she just pretending?

There is one dresses just like this

To go nowhere

He knows

He followed it

And found she walked always to a single place

One paving stone

And then came back

YOU COULDN'T BE JEALOUS OF THAT

She senses his loathing

It stiffens her cheek

She senses his heat

It awkwards her hips

HE WOULD BAWL AT ANYONE WHO COULD MAKE LOVE

Or argue a decent argument

Which also might be love

The ecstacy of the slap

The longing in the blow

She passes

Her rhythm grows faint

He feels his heart strain

To confront the hired space again

The room

The weight of the self in the ribs!

10

The intellectual in the moated manor
(Who dares to ridicule the moat
Is our violence not also medieval?)
Wrote in a miniature hand
(Knowing his bound books would become
Icons in foreign universities)
This translation of the Emperor Calipsius

PEOPLE RARELY SPEAK

Believing he had deciphered it afresh
This enigmatic assertion of antiquity
Chiming with his own belief that
Communication remained unfree
Because of bad social relations
And he wrote in imitation

PEOPLE WILL FIND VOICES

He felt proximity to emperors
Being walled round by power
              the violence of his judgement
              the pageantry of his reputation
              his corps of captive minds
Wearing thin purple in the summer
And as if to share the Dalmatian's pain
He suffered at the persistence of light planes
As Calipsius squirmed at wagon wheels
(The emperor ordained all streets
Within one mile of him be paved in felt)

But students he welcomed on Sundays after 2
Controlling their waywardness by contempt
And writing with a trowel

LIFE IS TOO BRIEF FOR BAD IDEAS TO BE DEBATED

In the summerhouse floor in wet cement
And if they argued past a certain point
He walked away
His
     sandals
          hissing
               between
                    staked
                        roses

His authority enhanced by loathing of civility
His disdain for opposition characterful

He required an audience
As a man examining his anus
Requires a mirror

11

You can lend too much room to opposition

The idea
The injudicious figment
The pernicious dogma
All men should be heard

INCLUDING FOOLS?

The child killer has cogent theories on taxation
The retired torturer
Distant from the shuttered shed
Colonial dust and
Bloody vests
Has a quiet voice in which he articulates
Every man's right to further education

YOU CAN'T LET EVERYONE TALK IMAGINE IT

The man with the cruel eye may drive the bus
But
Spare
Me
His
Logic
Says the party hack

The woman with the purple legs thinks wayward
Husbands should be branded with a maltese cross

Infants should be left on the beach overnight
The Darwinian motor mechanic opines at dusk

The necessity to make sense of plethora
Given our multitudes
To essay judgement
Given our variety

To choose to emphasize
Or wilfully neglect
The cogent and imperative

IF ONLY TRUTH WERE STABLE

The red-throated man is not more passionate
Nor is the silent man more sensitive
Nor the woman who laid her arguments
As perfect as the bricks of old palace walls
More trustworthy

Her compassionate expression
Her plump rejection of sin
Her jumpers proclaiming the maternity of breasts
Are also art

So we assess
And
Tirelessly assess

12

The painter's mistress acquiring cancer
He abandoned her
And she had half-created him

The poet of the working class
Placed his legs across the tracks
He had always loved trains

The playwright whose name was a household word
Shot himself in the temple
He had used the pistol in a film

You could not be both a painter and a nurse

You could not tolerate more separations

You could not create for a committee

13

Every man's death diminishes me

This

    You

        Might

            Utter

                In

                    Excess

                            Of

                                Faith

To affirm the sentimental cannot
To reiterate the doctrinal might not
Damage

But wholeness remains the harder thing
Bitter as probing the calyx of wounds

Old vagrant from whose nostrils pour twin streams
Who swallows snot with soup
And thereby demonstrates the ultimate economy

Shall I be you

Is an observation of the primer only
The springing of self from corruption

Young warder maddened by the club
Who shakes saliva on the brimming bruise
And thereby demonstrates the ultimate profligacy

Do I not also live in you

Is the point of departure
The locking of self to the wheel

Where

        Else

                Can

                        Wholeness

                                Lie

                                    But

                                        In

                                            This

Every man's evil expresses me

14

Her overall contained her

As plastic bags straining

From the fruiterer

Her laughter

Rang me from routine

In lifts she led their bawdy

And in the canteen spun

To catch the looks

Pinned like butterflies

To her despotic arse

The lepidoptera of men's stalking stares

And in the yellow confection of her hair

Flinging back the neon strip

As burst waves shatter the sun

Her art

Her gift

Howled its brief triumph

Sister

Who

Held back the hour

On the knife-grinding stair

Sister

All language has broken in

All knowledge has fenced us apart

15

The Viennese professor's son

White

Prematurely

White

Leaned down the heaving hills

Like the dog at the leash

All jaw

All fang

Like the police dog in its harness

An implosion of lung

The strapping of breath

The flinging saliva of unspent power

To the oily town which rebukes impatience

With its ranks of regular bricks

He lobs defiance

Shouting at the peopled wall

The roosted shelves of city cliffs

BEAUTY IS INSURRECTIONARY

(Insurrection being beautiful sounded

Dull now as the clapper on the

Cracked ton bell)

The Viennese professor's son

Red eyed

Invariably

Red eyed

When his dams burst and shook the towers

Of debate

Felt he could execute the race

And toss the warrants in the air

A cloud of falling archives

Drifting down among the cattle

Or clinging to matted buttocks

Of the sheep

34

As for pity

That

Blunt

Stick

Every cringing and fallen enemy

Wields against the just man's temper

Pity

What pity did you show the

Children

Did your victims not have children too

The trigger would never be denied

Its perfect exertion

He dreamed snows which half concealed

The rags of internationalists

35

And civil wars slanting like rains

Across the frontiers of infant states

The Viennese professor's son

Stooping

Prematurely

Stooping

Listens to the milkfloat crawl

Over pitted estates

The empties chorusing

The empties like lost generations

Squealing in their crates

This rushing gutter

This roaring pavement

He stops and slots his fingers in his ears

His hour might not come

The crowd might never cease its drift

16

This word stranger

Dissolves in deprivation
       in uprising
       in imminence of death

            the starved share a grating
            the looters bear away a fridge
            the howl of the bomb drove them
            to embrace

Carbonizes in property
       in repression
       in predation

            the neighbours joined but only to
            identify the sullen
            the opinion perished for fear of
            denunciation
            the man observes the child at play
            too long

This word stranger

17

The stranger's child
Usurping and imperative
Annexed all functions

Her body yielded all authority
As the servile instinct offers
Its poverty to the invader

Its mutiny
Its silent haste
Its fervid preparation

A gun stripped of its covers
A ship trimmed for its voyage
A house thrown open to the guest

The morning unto evening repetition
Which had made her weep some nights
Now shot into a cherished past

And her mind cried halt to transformation
Idiotically
Issued dictats to the deaf

A queen in a tower
Idiotic
To the boiling river of the crowd

Until considering her position
(She was not young)
Evaluating the prospect

(She might not love again)
Acknowledging the enthusiasm
Of her flesh
Her temper was appeased

Any man might be my husband
And any child my daughter
The blowing of the wind brought him
The effect of the broken span
The consequence of the power line's
Collapse

His breath was sometimes stale
And sometimes sweet
He made love like all men
The crowd moved in and out of him
A tide

This word stranger

18

The impotence of opinion

        its brief passage

The quickly mulching slogan

        its headlong autumn

Where the trams congregate

The elbows of the queue

Polish the bollard brighter than armour

In the cloister the toe of the saint

Has been kissed to a phalange of iron

She was a martyr of the nation

Now she brings husbands to girls

The teacher made many mistakes

And was reproved

Her silver head

Her seized shoulder

Over the square she goes crablike

Error gnawing her bones

The cobbles knew her better states

The rails once snatched her costly heels

The relative instability of politics

Is not sufficient reason to

Being born into an irrational era

Is no pretext for

And is drawn with such slowness up the hill

As if the weight of unkind memory

Would part the cable of persistent life

41

The uniforms!

The sheer incontinence of uniforms!

Splashed down on avenues

Grey petals blown

And drifting into sun-blind corners

Here the Russian lay six weeks

MARRY YOUR ENEMIES

But that is universal practice

FEED YOUR FOES

Is that not the rule of every kitchen

The German in her cellar turned

First red then blue

It was her lot

To live through nineteen governments

Obliging her to apologize nineteen times

It was her lot

To visit police stations as rich men visit clubs

To recant

To testify

To criticize

To denounce

To take refuge

To emerge from hiding

It was her lot

She fell across the corpse of the militiaman and laughed

Wonderful peal in the park

If she betrayed

Do you not think she also once believed?

19

The sane man
The sane woman
You ask how these shall be made

The kind man
The kind woman
You calculate their production

The kind man married the sane woman
And of their union came a silent child

Who walked through museums
Looking neither right nor left

Not registering the rotted gas mask
Nor the Etruscan wedding cup

Passing under the mammoth tusks
And between the colossal feet of
The Assyrian

The innocent heart of the howitzer
The boom of the prisoners' printing press

    She had no temper to explore
    No pain to bless
    Or rinse the inanimate in

20

The sallow comrade might imagine

The florid priest might dream

Passing between the shoppers who in

The moment of consumption

Experienced a slight relief

The imperialism of the soul

And its smudged banners

Parting the violent

Excusing the coarse

Funnelled down the aisles of the fruit market

Whose colours painted them with health

One rose to the slice of the abbey stair

While the other propped in the porch

Speaking together of

      manors of peace

      colonnades of tranquillity

and consciences silent as

the vaults of Norman keeps

Sleeps of such depths as come

To him who can dissolve his soul

In the greater soul of the people

As the grain of salt is shaken in the glass

Or the invisible will of the shoal

The perfect exhaustion of the correct choice

Being the antidote to

restless introspection

the pursuit of futile goals

preferring the short to the long term

petulance

incurring debts

moods and

casting away the love you engendered

as the drunk kicks off her shoe

high over the car roof

Have you watched the crowd on the stage
The way the crowd is made on the stage
Hundred legged knot of riot
Hundred handed hailers of autocracy

Have you watched the crowd on the film
The way the crowd is used on the film
The peasants grappling with books
The factory girls with their rifles

A mask of laughter thrust like a pie
On the furrowed surface of pains

                    the director's notes
                    the author's syntax

          drip
                  like
                      rain

Who dares to smother their histories?

Mother
Console your infant's dawning knowledge
She alarms the terrace in her cot

Old mother
Place your rumpled hand on your son's balding head
Part your daughter's greying streams
With fingers smooth from folding

Look
We pass in and out of one another
We pass in and out